Joseph and His Brothers

Award Publications Limited

Long ago, a good man called  lived in the land of Canaan. His many sons looked after the family's  and . One day, he gave his favourite son, , a fine  of many colours. This made the other  very jealous.

They also hated  because of his dreams, which showed him ruling over the family.

One day,  sent  to see if his  were keeping the  and the  safe in the wilderness.

The brothers saw  coming in his fine  of many colours.

"Let us kill him," they said. Reuben begged them not to, so they took the  and left  in a  to die. But Reuben planned to rescue him.

The other  were resting at an  near the  when a  came by. Judah said, "Let us sell  to these traders." The others agreed, so  was taken from the  and led away with the  to be sold as a slave in Egypt.

Then the  killed a , put its blood on the  of many colours and took it back to . He thought wild animals must have killed  and was full of grief.

In Egypt,  became the slave of , captain of the .

He worked very hard, and this pleased  so much that he made  head of his servants.

The wife of  fell in love with , but when  rejected her, she told lies to her husband about . So   threw  in prison.

In prison,  was able to explain the meaning of dreams to two servants of . Later, when  himself had strange dreams, he sent for  to explain them.

 told , "I saw seven thin  eating up seven fat , and seven thin ears of  eating

seven fat ears of ." Then  asked  to explain the dreams.

So  explained that seven years of good  would be followed by seven years of bad .

"What can I do?"  asked.

 replied, "Put a wise man in charge of the  so that enough is stored in the good years to feed everyone in the years of bad ."

Then   said, "I see that God is with you," and he commanded  to take charge of the grain in Egypt.

The work  did pleased .

He gave him a  and a gold .

For seven years,  stored the , so that the people would have food when the  was bad.

Then, during the bad years the  came to Egypt to buy food.

 knew them at once, but they

did not recognise  .

"Why are you here?" he asked them.

"We have come to buy food because there is none in our land," answered the . But  pretended not to believe them.

"You are spies," he said, and he told his  to put them in prison.

After three days,  set his  free. He sent them all back to their father, , except Simeon.

"Return with your brother, ," said , "or I will have Simeon put to death."

But  was unwilling for his youngest son, , to go to Egypt. "I have already lost !" cried . "I cannot now lose !"

Yet the people needed food, so in the end  had to send  back with his brothers.  wept tears of joy when  arrived.

So  released Simeon and sold his  all the food they needed. As their  was about to leave,  ordered a servant to hide a silver  inside the  belonging to .

When the  had left,  sent the  after their .

The  was found. "So  must stay as my servant," said .

But Judah pleaded with  "No, take me as your slave instead."

"Let  and my other  go home," he begged.  could not pretend any more, and told his  who he really was. They were amazed.

"Go back to ," said , "and bring him and all his family, and the  and , here to live with me in Egypt."

And so  was reunited with , and all of the , and the family lived happily together in Egypt.

You can find out all about this story in the Bible:
Genesis 37–50

ISBN 978-1-78270-657-1

Copyright © Award Publications Limited

Illustrated by Pamela Johnson

All rights reserved. No part of this publication may be reproduced or utilised in any form or by any means electronic or mechanical, including photocopying, recording, or by any information storage and retrieval system now known or hereafter invented, without the prior written permission of the publisher.

This edition first published 2025

Published by Award Publications Limited,
The Old Riding School, Welbeck,
Worksop, S80 3LR

/awardpublications @award.books
www.awardpublications.co.uk

24-1148 1

Printed in China